KPIS

A NEW APPROACH

ROBERTSON HUNTER STEWART

KPIs
A NEW APPROACH

The author of this work is:

Robertson Hunter Stewart
Born 1962, St Andrews, Scotland

TABLE OF CONTENTS

KPIs

A NEW APPROACH

INTRODUCTION

In today's fast-paced and complex business world, organisations are constantly looking for ways to measure their success and track their progress in order to identify sustainable sources of competitive advantage.

Traditionally, key performance indicators (KPIs) have focused on metrics, measuring revenue, profits, market share and competitiveness, all of which are undeniably important. These measurements are, if you like, the visible manifestations of how the company or organisation performs and give some indication as to whether or not it is well run. They give us information in comparison to a number of given objectives and expectations, and help us make informed business decisions based on our interpretation of the results.

What they do not do is tell us exactly how we arrived at the given results or what enabled us to do so. They are, in fact, only at the very tip of the proverbial iceberg.

If we consider that, all else being equal, we have access to the same material, financial, physical and intangible resources, what is it that allows us to perform better than we did last year or compared to our competition in our marketplace? The answer is quite simple. The variable that we are looking for is **people!**

Although people should be considered as more than mere assets, we could say it is our people who allow us to manipulate and transform all of the previously mentioned assets in order to produce goods and services for our customers. Furthermore, it is people who will give us the opportunity to create and sustain an eventual competitive advantage in the marketplace.

Employee-centric KPIs recognise that the people who work for a company or organisation are by far its most important resource.

USING KPIs EFFECTIVELY

As leaders, we all know and constantly use the more common KPIs that suit whatever business or industry we are in, whether it is primary (extraction of raw materials), secondary (manufacturing) or tertiary (service sector) in nature. From measuring productivity to measuring the satisfaction of our clients or the profitability of our organisation, we always need a certain number of **indicators** that are more important than others in determining the **performance** – the progress or success – of our business, which is exactly why they become **key**.

Typically, a business will have a variety of KPIs which are designed to measure its overall performance, and then further KPIs to measure the results of a number of areas within the business such as production, finance, sales and marketing, research and development, human resources and quality control. Whatever areas we use

KPIs for in our business, they must always have two things in common. First, they have to be measurable, and secondly, they need to have a point of comparison.

To explain this, let's take an example from finance. Let's say that we are measuring the financial performance of our business and have decided to look at profitability. Furthermore, we are measuring the level of gross operating profit (GOP) made by the company calculated as a percentage of the overall sales.

At first glance, this may look to be a very simple example. However, we have to make a number of decisions, such as what exactly are the total sales we'll use? Do they include or exclude certain sales or value added tax?

Once we have decided this, we divide the GOP by the total sales for the period in question (a week, a month, a year) and represent the result as a percentage. We can calculate this fairly easily. What is extremely important, though, is that it always needs to be calculated in exactly the same way every time we measure this KPI, so that we can compare apples with apples. We now have to decide what we are going to use as the point of comparison.

If we have obtained the result for the whole year in our example and this result is 35%, this means that the GOP for the year represents 35% of the sales for that period. However, on its own, this result has absolutely no significance whatsoever, apart from the fact that the calculation has been done correctly. In order for it to mean something, we have to have a point of reference. In this case, we have the choice between several, for example our result of 35% compared to last year, compared to the last forecast, to the budget, to the industry standard.

In other words, we have to decide whether the result is good or bad, and compared to what. For example, our result might be OK compared to budget, but less than for the same period last year. Alternatively, we might be looking at a result that is better than last year *and* our budget, but it is five percentage points behind the industry average, which stands at 40%. If this is the case, it indicates poor performance compared to our competition.

Moreover, we need to look at the result in relation to other results if it is to have any real meaning or even be useful. 35% might be better than last year and the year before. It might even be better than the industry average, but if our sales are only 10% of last year's, we might still find ourselves bankrupt because we are not in a position to pay our suppliers or the salaries of our employees.

In other words, 35% of nothing is still nothing. This is why we need to have several KPIs for our business or organisation before we will be in a position to make judgements concerning whether or not the overall business is performing well and is competitive.

But we don't only need to *have* KPIs in order to know how our business is performing. We also need to make sure that we measure the right things in the right way.

So, how exactly do we go about choosing what we need to measure? To answer this question, let's use an example that I often use with management and leadership students.

Imagine an airline pilot. In the cockpit, an airline pilot has a very large number of instruments and measures which they need to take into account if they are to reach their predetermined destination without incident. However, there are measures which they *always* need to take into account, whatever the type of aircraft they are flying and wherever their destination might be. So, what are the key measurements that need to be monitored by the pilot?

I'm by no means an expert (or a pilot), but for me, all of the following are key measurements:

> The altitude of the aircraft
> How much fuel the aircraft has
> The speed of the aircraft
> The air pressure inside the aircraft
> The attitude of the aircraft

It's probably obvious, but if any of the above are incorrectly measured, or measured at the wrong time, the results for the pilot, the crew and the passengers will likely be catastrophic.

Of course, you don't have to be an airline pilot to understand the importance of having a certain number of critical measurements. Driving a car is a good example. While travelling along, you are constantly checking your speed and your mirrors to ensure that you are not endangering yourself or others. Before setting off, you check that you have enough fuel in the car to get from point A to point B. You adjust the temperature in the vehicle to one that is comfortable (not too hot, not too cold). You check the tyre pressure to ensure that you can drive safely and don't use too much fuel. You keep your eye on the temperature gauge so that the engine does not become too hot – if it does, stop the car and get out before it bursts into flames!

In both cases (flying the aircraft and driving the car), there are a number of critical things you have to constantly and consistently measure to ensure that you reach the primary objective of your journey. In other words, your KPIs on this occasion allow you to arrive safely at your destination.

Running, or "piloting", a business is the same. You need to have a certain number of well-chosen and relevant KPIs to ensure that you run your business in the optimum way to become or stay both profitable and, of course, ahead of the competition.

The precise choice of your KPIs will depend to a large extent upon the industry that you are in and the amount of competition in your market, as well as the mission, vision, goals and objectives of your organisation. Once again, let's take an example that many of you will be familiar with to demonstrate a relevant set of KPI measurements. Let's look at a hotel.

Imagine that one of the KPIs of the hotel is room occupancy and another is the average daily room rate paid by the customers. The hotel in question has 100 rooms, of which 80 are occupied at the moment. So, the occupancy of the hotel is at 80%. As the owner or manager of the premises, you could regard this as quite good, right? It is in actual fact not bad, but there is another vital piece of information you need before you can say whether or not this is healthy perfor- mance from a financial point of view.

What about the price each guest has paid for the room? If you sell 80 rooms for $10 per night, you are not going to make much money. On the other hand, if you sell 80 rooms at the price of $200 per night, you would make $16,000 as opposed to a mere $800.

This illustrates once again why we often need several indicators in order to obtain results which actually mean something and enable us to draw conclusions and base decisions on these observations.

THE HUMAN ELEMENT

Whether we are driving a car, piloting an aeroplane or running a business, we still require human intervention (in spite of current progress with artificial intelligence (AI)). There are two things to consider in this regard. First of all, how **skilled the person is at interpreting the results** and making necessary adjustments to improve their performance. Secondly, **where have the results come from and how have they been produced**? In both cases, the questions are **who** has produced and influenced the results and in **what way**? In other words, what is it that really ensures whether we get good results or not?

Let's take a look at a Grand Prix race. There will be two main factors which will determine who wins the race. The first factor is how good the car is and the second will be how good the driver is. You do, of course, need to have a good car *and* a good driver if you want to give yourself the best chance of winning. A great car with a poor driver is not likely to win, and neither is a poor car, however good the driver is.

But how did the racing car get built? Who imagined, designed and constructed it? At each stage, people will have been involved. Whether it was computer assisted or not, the design still required human intervention. In the production of the car, robots might have played a huge part, but they still needed to be programmed correctly by human hands. When the performance of the car is being tested, you need a team to maintain it properly at a number of different levels. So, the car's ultimate performance in a race will come down not only to how good the driver is, but also to how good all of the people involved in designing, building and maintaining it are.

This same analogy holds true, no matter what kind of company, business or organisation we are involved with. Different levels of performance and whether the company does or doesn't become competitive in a sustainable way depends on the quality of the people involved, their level of competence and how motivated they are to win.

We often have a lot of different people and areas of expertise involved in our attempt to win (and keep) our competitive advantage. However, this advantage can only be sustained if our people are **informed, involved, interested** and **inspired**. These are the truly fundamental and actionable KPIs, the hidden part of the iceberg that will actually allow performance to become apparent, improve and be measurable with the traditional types of KPIs we discussed earlier.

To positively influence the outcomes for the metrics of **employee satisfaction, engagement** and **retention**, we need to build on the most solid foundations possible. Not simply by taking note of these metrics and giving them the importance that they truly deserve, but even more crucially by working on fundamental reasons for people's success as human beings within organisations today. So, the truly key KPIs are:

KEEP PEOPLE INFORMED
KEEP PEOPLE INVOLVED
KEEP PEOPLE INTERESTED
KEEP PEOPLE INSPIRED

This book will discuss how the new approach to KPIs will become the most important driving force behind an era of inspirational leadership. It will help businesses and organisations reach previously unknown levels of performance. It will clearly demonstrate that the new KPIs are not designed to replace the more traditional ones, but to be used in tandem with them to produce exceptional results.

KEEP PEOPLE INFORMED

WHY KEEP PEOPLE INFORMED?

Communicating effectively with your people is vital in your organisation for a number of different reasons.

It enhances collaboration and creates an environment in which mutual understanding of objectives encourages individuals to work together towards common goals. Optimum levels of communication between team members also fosters effective teamwork and reduces the likelihood of conflict.

Good, effective communication facilitates the sharing of ideas, information and knowledge between team members and different teams within the organisation, effectively avoiding the "silo effect" (employees working only on their own or their department's objective and not taking any notice of or interest in what is going on elsewhere). Common access to information and knowledge ensures that people stay on course with regard to the common objectives and the mission of the organisation.

In other words, great communication allows you to properly align your people throughout the entire organisation with the vision, mission and values of your company.

The way that you as leader communicate within the organisation helps build trust and cooperation between team members, as well as between you and each individual. This in turn will lead to a more positive and productive work environment where the psychological safety of people at all levels can and will be assured.

Furthermore, if you wish your organisation to be innovative and effective in building its capacity for problem solving, excellent communication is a must. You are likely to have heard the expression "two heads are better than one". This is true, but you will only benefit fully from this concept with great communication across the organisation.

As a manager and/or leader, you are likely to understand why effective communication is essential to the long-term wellbeing of your employees and the organisation as a whole. However, it is vital that everyone around you understands the overall goals and culture of the organisation of which they are a part. Communicating your goals and culture correctly avoids people pulling in diametrically opposed directions, allowing the organisation to remain both whole and wholesome, and giving it a real chance of being competitive in today's volatile, complex and sometimes unstable environment.

However, understanding why it's important and knowing how to go about effectively keeping your people informed are two entirely different things. Let's now take a look at just how to ensure effective communication within your organisation to keep your people informed.

HOW TO KEEP PEOPLE INFORMED

KEYWORD – COMMUNICATION

First and foremost, let's state the obvious! The best way of keeping people informed is by talking to them.

Do remember, though, that when you talk to your people, you also have to take time to listen. Quite simply, if you talk to people in a way that makes whatever you're saying interesting to them, and really listen to their responses, you will foster effective communication.

However, in order to ensure and maintain this type of effective communication, you need to create multiple opportunities to do so. In other words, to communicate effectively, set aside the appropriate amount of time to do it properly. You won't engender anything but impatience and exasperation if you're constantly checking your watch while your team members are responding to whatever you've been talking about.

You may keep people informed in lots of different ways, for example through briefings, one-to-one meetings, coaching, mentoring and written and electronic information channels. Whatever medium you choose, the most important thing is that the channel of communication remains open and effective.

What do I mean by open and effective? To better understand this, let's take the example of parents communicating with their teenage children. At the time of writing, I am 60 and my son is 18. On one occasion, after having tried several times over an extended period to contact him by telephone with absolutely no success whatsoever, I tried an SMS. Guess what? He answered almost immediately. This demonstrates that although the channel of speakingon the telephone was available, it was neither opennor effective.

Let's take another example. Imagine an operations briefing in a workplace situation. Normally, the shift leader would brief his or her people before the beginning of every shift to give them all the updates and information they need to complete their tasks without incident. Let's say that the briefing normally takes five minutes with a couple of minutes for a question and answer session at the end. People in the shift leader's team have accepted this as the modus operandi.

However, recently the shift leader has started stretching out the briefings and talking more and more about HR and overall company issues. Some of this information may be important to his or her team members, but is the pre-shift briefing the right time to share it?

Under these circumstances, it's likely that some of the people on the team might not only fail to absorbthe information, but actually become disinterested or even bored because the briefing is no longer opera-tional in nature. The channel of communication may still be open, but it is not as effective as it should be. Quite simply, although all of the information is important, the shift leader is using the wrong channel to share it.

TEAM MEETINGS

A team meeting can be a good time to ensure that information is passed on to people. Once again, however, this has to be done in the right way with respect to a certain number of "rules" if the channel is to remain both open and effective.

One rule that is absolutely fundamental, but often forgotten, is that team meetings must take place throughout the entire organisation at much the same frequency and contain the same information outside of what is job or role specific. Why is this so critical? Quite simply, if the level and content of information given to people differs from one part of the organisation to another, this will lead to breakdowns in communication between services and departments. Ultimately, this runs the risk of departments operating in silo mode, becoming competing mini-organisations within the organisation.

The good news is there are simple ways to avoid this. One is to **make meetings an objective for supervisory and management staff** at all levels in the organisation. For example, ask all managers to carry out structured team meetings on a monthly basis and provide meeting minutes as part of their yearly appraisal process.

Successful meetings are based on the following principles:

> - The right people are invited
> - People are informed of the meeting in good time
> - The meeting has an agenda and a purpose

> ➤ The meeting is structured
> ➤ Minutes from previous meeting(s) are made available to all attendees before the next meeting

Let's take a look at these points one at a time. Inviting the right people is obvious in the sense that you want to be giving pertinent information to those who attend the meeting. You probably know what it's like to sit through a meeting that has absolutely nothing to do with you and your role, finding yourself praying for the coffee break or the end of the meeting to bring your suffering to a close. You know what I'm talking about, right?

If informing people during a meeting is important, it's equally important to let them know when the meeting is going to take place well in advance. Don't forget that you are not the only one in the organisation with a busy schedule. This advance notice allows people to be prepared for the meeting so they can actually look forward to it rather than dread it.

If you've ever been invited to a meeting at the last minute, you'll know what I mean. You have no time to prepare and feel put on the spot during the meeting, which as a result feels more like a punishment than anything else.

Giving people the necessary time to prepare is essential if you want your meetings to be both constructive and effective. This goes hand in hand with ensuring that the people invited to the meeting have access to the agenda well in advance as it gives them the opportunity to plan and prepare properly.

When I say that meetings should be structured, I am referring to two things. First of all, the agenda will outline the subjects to be discussed and usually the order in which they will be dealt with. However, attendees also need to know exactly what role they are going to play in the meeting. Who is going to run the meeting? Who is going to be in charge of timekeeping? Who is going to take the minutes? To what extent is each individual expected to participate?

An interesting tactic in my experience is to change who chairs the meetings from time to time. This gives people the opportunity to gain experience and is extremely useful to observe when you are planning succession (i.e. who to train for promotion for roles up to and including your own).

Last but not least, all of the participants need to have access to the minutes of previous meetings. This ensures that attendees don't end up discussing the same matters over and over again, unless of course there is a particular reason to do so.

All these points may seem blatantly obvious when they are explained like this. Nevertheless, I am sure that during your career, you've seen how horribly wrong a meeting can go if one of these essential ingredients is skipped or not followed properly. Basically, if you believe that your people need to be informed, ensure that they receive information in the most effective and efficient way possible. That, of course, means ensuring that everyone is engaged and involved in every meeting they attend.

In today's world, meetings are often held remotely via platforms such as Microsoft Teams, Zoom or even Skype for some of us Baby Boomers! However, the same rules apply as for meetings where people are physi- cally present. All meetings need all the criteria we have discussed in this section.

Having a quick chat on Zoom is exactly the same as having an informal chat with one of your employees next to the coffee machine. It might be a necessary social courtesy, but it cannot replace planned and formal meetings. It really is only a "virtual coffee".

To ensure that you are not just having a virtual coffee when you're holding a remote meeting, here are some tips:

> Use the right channel to host the meeting. There is a lot of choice today, with Zoom and Microsoft Teams currently being the most reliable
> Do the tech check before the meeting. In other words, make sure that all participants have a good internet connection and that their audio and video are working before the meeting
> Ask all attendees to leave their cameras on during the meeting as this improves the ambiance and leads to more effective commu- nication. A large part of communication is non-verbal in nature
> Introduce a meeting protocol, outlining for example when microphones are to be mutedand unmuted to avoid unwanted background noise. Ensure that people know they can

> unmute whenever they wish in order to foster active participation
> ➢ Cut screen-share presentations down to the minimum and plan your meetings more around discussion and dialogue
> ➢ Make virtual meetings shorter than face-to-face meetings. Personally, I would recommend one hour as an absolute maximum
> ➢ Don't forget to record your meetings so that the recording can act as the minutes and be sent to participants afterwards (either as it is or in the form of a podcast)

These points will help ensure that your virtual meetings take on a more human aspect and remain as participative and effective as possible.

ONE-TO-ONE COMMUNICATION

We have discussed how best to inform your teams through operational briefings or structured monthly departmental meetings. However, there are certain types of information that need to be given, received and discussed on an individual basis. Two extremely important examples of this channel of communication are the yearly evaluation or appraisal interviews, and one-to-one meetings with your direct reports.

Both of these types of meeting are critical to the successful sharing of information relevant only to the person in question. You will often discuss departmental and operational KPIs with your team members here, but you'll also include their individual objectives. Personal development, areas of potential improvement and the identification of training needs are fundamental areas to discuss during one-to-one sessions.

These meetings are great opportunities to listen to each team member and give constructive feedback on issues relative to his or her performance, behaviour and development needs. Nevertheless, remember that you are not obliged to agree on every single issue you discuss. After all, disagreement is not the same as conflict, far from it. Disagreement can lead to some very healthy outcomes. Conflict, on the other hand, often proves costly to everyone involved and to the organisation as a whole. Always remember to mark the difference between the two.

If you and a team member disagree on a specific subject, ensure that you both have adequate time to air your views. This will not only enhance effective communication between you and your reports as they feel safe to give their honest opinion, it also dramatically increases the chances of you finding a consensus and moving forward.

As I'm sure you can imagine, constructive and well-structured one-to-one meetings are critical to sharing information with individuals, so make every effort to hold them frequently. With my own direct reports, I have found the optimum frequency to be monthly, and the optimum length is between one and one-and-a-half hours.

Regard regular one-to-one meetings as privileged moments for both the manager and employee. They're crucial milestones between last year's and this year's annual performance reviews that avoid unfortunate and unwelcome surprises for all concerned at the end of the year. They also mean any issues can be discussed and resolved to the satisfaction of both parties before they become major problems.

WRITTEN COMMUNICATION

So far, we have discussed how to keep people informed verbally via either **one-to-many** or **one-to-one** meetings, although we have included the importance of the written word in agendas and meeting minutes. However, written methods of sharing information go far beyond these essential tools.

There are so many ways to pass on written information that I am not even going to try to list them all here. I will simply discuss those that I believe to be the most important today.

Remember my earlier example of having to send an SMS to my son in order to obtain a response? Whatever vehicle of communication you decide to use, you must ensure two things: that the vehicle is adopted by the majority of your employees, and that it is effective for its chosen purpose.

It is undeniable that the use of technology has become prevalent in communication and the sharing of information, both in everyday life and, to an even greater extent, in today's workplace. This can go from sending an email to using dedicated workplace social media channels, from building an intranet for your employees to sending out electronic newsletters, and all the way to using WhatsApp groups to ensure communication during a crisis.

Let's elaborate on this last point. If you were to use email to inform company executives of a crisis situa- tion such as a fire having broken out in the workplace, this would not have the desired level of urgency. Many people only check their email at certain times, so it's likely they wouldn't learn this crucial information until it was out of date. On the other hand, informing them through a WhatsApp group (having already evacuated the building and called the fire brigade, of course), you will be far more likely to receive an immediate response.

My advice to you is to take the time to choose the right vehicles of communication for your organisation. Make the decision on which to use with the people you lead to ensure that the vehicles are adopted by everyone in the organisation and they all, including management and leadership teams, know how to use them (do not assume this). Then **inform everyone** about the channels of communication that are preferred within the organisation.

To demonstrate the importance of this point, imagine that you have informed all of your employees that as of today, every person in the organisation, including those who work from home, will receive a formal performance review which is structured, well designed and takes into account each of their personal objectives, as well as giving constructive feedback on individual training and development needs. Sounds great, doesn't it? Until you discover that you have neglected to train your managers and leaders on how to carry out remote appraisal interviews via the organisation's preferred vehicle of communication.

This brings us neatly to the last point about keeping people informed. Always ensure to the best of your ability that the information you share is correct, relevant and up to date. Relevance is extremely important so that all the **right people** have all the **right information** at the **right time.**

Remember:

"Communication – the human connection – is the key to personal and career success."

Paul J Meyer[1]

Now that you have access to all of the necessary communication channels and skills, let's take a closer look at how to keep your people as **involved** as possible with what's going on in their place of work.

KEEP PEOPLE INVOLVED

WHY KEEP PEOPLE INVOLVED?

Keeping people involved with their work is essential to success for many different reasons. Foremost among them are purpose, motivation and engagement. It may sound obvious, but it can be overlooked by business leaders: when people are highly involved with the work that they are doing, their sense of purpose, motivation and engagement will be heightened.

Under these circumstances, it stands to reason that your team members will take an active interest in improving their own performance in terms of not only productivity, but also the quality of the work they produce. In other words, if you consider purpose, motivation and engagement as important inputs, the outputs will be better overall productivity and quality of work within the organisation as a whole. This often leads to a situation where your team members will be open to learning and developing new skills, which reinforces the positive outcomes.

This is critical today with the recruitment, selection and retention of talent becoming more and more strategic, particularly when we look at trends such as the great resignation (where large groups of employees resign from their jobs) and/or quiet quitting (employees doing the minimum required of them and no more). If we as managers and leaders do not do whatever is necessary to involve our people so they become active participants in the life of the organisation, we are going to spend a lot of time and money running after talent instead of nurturing it.

We all know deep down that if we are extremely involved and happy in what we are doing, this will contribute not only to our own wellbeing, but also towards building a healthy culture in a workplace where everyone will feel empowered to take a certain amount of risk. This risk will lead to higher levels of creativity and innovation, both of which are essential when we're setting up our organisation to become successful.

If you wish to foster environments where everyone feels motivated and engaged and will truly thrive – and I'm guessing you do – you must do everything possibleto encourage the active participation of all of your employees. You need to look at all the different ways in which you can help your employees actively partic-ipate on an ongoing basis to the life and success of the organisation.

So, it's obvious that all your people need to be involved with your organisation if it is to succeed. Let's now take a look at just how to go about this.

HOW TO KEEP PEOPLE INVOLVED

KEYWORD – PARTICIPATION

Let's look at one of the closing sentences from the previous chapter. Relevance is extremely important so that all the **right people** have all the **right information** at the **right time.**

If you want people to be involved in what they are doing within your organisation and participate as much as possible at work, it's a prerequisite that what they are involved with is relevant to them in some way. Before going further, however, I should point out that this relevance does not necessarily have to have anything to do with their work. It can come from outside influences and often relates to our epoch and the challenges we all face globally as human beings.

You may have heard people say that we live in a VUCA world ("VUCA" being an acronym for volatile, uncertain, complex and ambiguous).[2] This concept takes on relevance when you look at current geo-political and environmental issues and concerns. At the time of writing, not the least of these is economic, with price inflation at extremely high levels. Then there are ongoing environmental concerns that affect us all, such as the dire consequences of global warming and massive reductions in biodiversity, with all the ensuing impacts on ecosystems.

These concerns impact each and every one of us, not only as individuals, but collectively as human beings, which means they must take on importance as part of today's organisational culture. If we as leaders wishto see people heavily involved with what our compa- nies and organisations are doing, we need a highly visible and serious approach to addressing these global concerns.

CORPORATE SOCIAL RESPONSIBILITY

For companies, concerns that affect the whole of humanity generally come under the umbrella of corporate social responsibility (CSR). If we wish our people to be involved in their work, we first need to take a very active interest in our approach to CSR.

There are three distinct parts of CSR: economic, environmental and social. Taking the economic part first, let's state the obvious once again: people must be remunerated for the work they do. This is an area that cannot be ignored by any employer. If we do so, it will in no way alleviate the current trends of quiet quitting and great resigning. Instead, we will risk suffering a higher than normal turnover within our organisation. This in turn will inevitably lead to higher than normal operational costs as we desperately try to recruit and train new talent.

As leaders and managers, we need to think further than just the salary. We need to look not only at whether the salaries our organisation offers are competitive, but also at whether they are keeping pace with inflation and allowing our people to enjoy continued access to disposable income.

Looking more globally, we need to ensure that our companies' financial results are visible. This is part of an organisation's fiduciary responsibility, but we also need to do this to ensure the continuing activity of the business and the stable employment that provides. In other words, financial visibility ensures the perennity of the organisation and reassures all the stakeholders in the business.

If we as leaders wish our employees to feel truly involved in our organisation, we have to ensure thatwe adapt to economic uncertainty by keeping in mind the wants and needs of the business globally. Even more importantly, we must consider the wants and needs of the people who run the business with us. Moreover, we must ensure transparency and honestyin this regard, particularly when we're dealing with sensitive discussions such as profit sharing among the various stakeholders or salary negotiations with employees (whether individual or global).

As a leader, take an active interest in your company's economic CSR. Showing that you care about your people's economic situation will foster high levels of investment and involvement from your employees.

Now let's move on to the environmental CSR. Changes in the environment are already affecting us in our personal lives. For example, certain areas of the US no longer have access to clean drinking water from taps.[3] Many of us are selectively sorting our garbage or reducing our personal carbon footprint where possible by using our cars less or changing the type of vehicle that we use on a daily basis. It is only natural, therefore, that our people will have high expectations of our companies and organisations in terms of what we are doing to make them environmentally sustainable.

Imagine that you are the manager of a restaurant. If you don't care at all about food wastage, selectively sorting garbage, using local producers and seasonal products to reduce your carbon footprint, everything else being equal (for example salary), you are going to find it more and more difficult to recruit or keep any employees, let alone those who are actively involved with your business. Conversely, if you have in place a solid vision about the environment and environmental standards (in other words, your organisation is as far removed from "greenwashing" – where you provide false evidence of it being eco-friendly – as humanly possible), you will be in a position to actively involve your people in your efforts. In fact, you will be able to do this to the point where your people not only respect your current standards, but make their own proposals on how to improve things and reduce the carbon footprint of the business.

Let's now take a look at the social part of the CSR equation. First and foremost, we all want to be treated well within the workplace. As a leader you definitely need to make one of your primary concerns ensuring the physical and psychological safety of your team members. In its simplest form, this means ensuring that people work in acceptable conditions where there are appropriate levels of lighting, heating and noise, and/ or equipment which reduces the impact of any of these.

Let's say that you have done everything possible to ensure maximum workplace safety and hygiene, and that procedures are in place to make this approach sustainable. If you are sincere in your wish to involve your people and allow them to thrive, you have to create an environment where they feel **psychologically** safe.

To achieve this, steer well clear of micromanaging. Let your people participate in the decision-making process, all the way from what kind of decorations to put in place during the Christmas season to actively participating in the choice of their personal objectives for the coming year. In this way, you will be sowing the seeds for more active participation and involvement within the organisation.

A SAFE WORKING ENVIRONMENT
IN A VUCA WORLD

So far, we've talked mainly about how to deal with our VUCA world from a global perspective through our efforts regarding our organisation's CSR policy. With regard to what I like to call the "VUCA equation", managers and leaders also have a more personal role to play.

Take the word **volatile** from the VUCA acronym. Within an organisation, relationships can very quickly become explosive in nature when misunderstandings occur. One of your primary skills as a leader is to be able to spot areas of contention and "demine" them before the explosion occurs. Obviously, if you **involve** people more in the running of the organisation, allowing them to participate on a regular basis and **informing** them frequently, you will be in a far better position to do this.

Uncertainty, the U of VUCA, is an ongoing problem for many of your people, often connected to worry regarding future events. Uncertainty in the workplace commonly manifests itself through questions such as "Am I going to keep my job? Can I adapt to the new working conditions? Am I going to be recognised for what I am doing or what I am capable of?" This last point about recognition is particularly important, so we'll come back to it in detail in the "Keep People Interested" chapter. The uncertainty your people feel often translates into anxiety, fear and, in certain cases, depression.

Here, your role as a leader will be to reduce the amount and severity of uncertainty in your organisation. You do this through consistent and healthy communication, and by building trust through keeping your promises. Say what you mean, mean what you say, and ensure that your actions reflect your words.

You can alleviate your people's fears by giving them reassurance as much as possible. Transparency lessens the root causes of uncertainty as your people will quickly realise they can trust you.

What about the C, the **complex** element of VUCA? Your people will often need to be able to solve complex problems related to their job and of a more general nature within the workplace. It's therefore crucial that you make sure they are in a position to do so, either by helping them directly or, even better, by giving them the tools that enable them to solve problems for themselves.

Remember:

"Give a man a fish, and you feed him for a day. Teach a man to fish and you feed him for a lifetime."

Adapted from the novel *Mrs Dymond* by Anna Isabella Thackeray Ritchie.[4]

My interpretation of this leads me to spend more time teaching my team members how to solve problems rather than solving each problem that comes along with them. For example, by equipping them with brainstorming techniques then taking a backseat in brainstorming sessions, I facilitate lively discussions, ideas, creativity and innovation.

Last but not least, **ambiguity**. Your job as a leader in this respect is to provide purpose and clarity through the vision you share with your people. It should bea given that you ensure your people learn and understand the overall objectives of the organisation during the induction or onboarding process. What I'm talking about here is your role as coach to your teams and the individuals in them. To avoid ambiguity, you need to be explicit in your everyday communication. It would be more than unfair to think anyone will be aligned with your expectations as their leader if you haven't made those expectations crystal clear.

As a leader, never rely on implicit understanding. Explain all the expectations you have, and then check with your people that they have fully understood these expectations. In this way, you will be actively promoting a healthy work culture where explicit communication and the right to ask questions are the norm.

This kind of healthy work culture, where people can thrive and find purpose and clarity, is paramount, particularly in a VUCA world. So, this bears repeating: always say what you mean, mean what you say and do whatever you said you would do. Remember, culture might be invisible, but like the wind, its effects are always felt, however strong or weak it is. As leader, you need to hold yourself accountable for guaranteeing a safe and healthy workplace culture if you truly wish people to participate of their own free will.

SMART OBJECTIVES

Let's now take a closer look at the importance of objectives. I'm sure you will have heard the acronym SMART to describe how to set goals and objectives.[5] The original version of the acronym stood for specific, measurable, attainable, realistic and timed. This is already a good framework for formulating goals and objectives with your team members, but my personal version of the acronym is:

➢ S – specific, simple, scope
➢ M – measurable
➢ A – achievable, agreed and ambitious
➢ R – relevant
➢ T – timed

As you can see, there are similarities and differences to the original here. Let's discuss the importance of the differences.

For the S, I have added simple and scope. Simple in this context means that the objective is easily understood by all parties. This does not mean that you cannot have an objective which is complex; what it means is that the objective must be simply, precisely and clearly explained. It also means that you as leader check in with the people receiving the objective to make sure they have understood thoroughly.

What about scope? Why even mention scope? Surely, it comes under being specific, doesn't it? No, not at all.

As a case in point, if someone were to ask you to build a house for them, that instruction would be specific in itself. You've not been asked to build a car, a caravan or a shed; the objective is specifically to build a house. However, in order for the objective to be achieved, you need to fill in a certain number of blanks. In other words, you need the scope, such as how many rooms will there be in the house? How many floors? What material will you use to build it? How many windows will it need? And so on. If you don't receive the scope of the objective, you might end up building a straw hut rather than a stone house.

For the A of SMART, attainable has changed to achievable, and there are two additions: agreed and ambitious. It stands to reason that if you really want your people to be thoroughly involved with what they are doing, you need to get their agreement on the objectives you wish to set rather than simply imposing them.

As for ambitious, this is not the opposite of achievable. What it means here is that you need to give your people at least a bit of a challenge or a problem to solve if you want to involve them in what they are doing. This is particularly true if you are dealing with high achievers in your team. If these people are not challenged in any way by the objectives you agree on, they're likely soon to be looking for a challenge elsewhere.

The R has been changed from realistic to relevant. Firstly, if something is achievable, it is realistic, so this point becomes superfluous. Secondly, and more importantly, the objective has to be relevant to the person you are agreeing it with. They have to have the relevant skills, competence, ability, and access to resources to have a fair chance of completing the objective in question. The objective also needs to be relevant, and therefore of interest, to the individual personally if they are going to be invested in achieving it.

If you concentrate on making sure that the objectives you agree with your team members are truly SMART, this will lead to a much better employee experience.

Your people will be more engaged not only with the objectives, but also with you as the leader and the organisation overall.

In this chapter, we've talked about increasing the involvement of your people by addressing global issues and allowing them to participate in the setting of objectives. Is that it? Not quite.

As a leader, you must find every possible opportunity to increase the participation of your employees. You can achieve this through the one-to-one or team meetings that we discussed in the previous chapter, and by allowing them to actively participate in problem solving through role playing, management by theatre and brainstorming. What is management by theatre? It is basically role playing specific situations which need to be managed, such as a crisis or how to deal with difficult or disciplinary actions.

In fact, there are a host of collaborative techniques which use methods based on collective intelligence. You can find more information about these techniques in my book *Employee Power*.[6]

Always remember that allowing people to participate is the key to them becoming more involved in the results of any collective effort. Whether it relates to their favourite sports team or the company they work for, active participation leads to maximum involvement.

KEEP PEOPLE INTERESTED

WHY KEEP PEOPLE INTERESTED?

It is of paramount importance to maintain the interest of your team, and the individuals that make it up, day in, day out.

I'm sure you know what it's like to lose interest in a hobby or pastime. This loss of interest can often lead to a situation where you don't quite know what to do with yourself in your free time. You are likely to have experienced this type of feeling at one time or another.

But just imagine how bad the feeling would be if it was the case at work! If you consider the amount of time that we all spend at work, it would be awful to have no real sense of purpose or interest in what you are doing most of the time, wouldn't it?

Conversely, when you are extremely interested in something, whether at or outside of work, it can often become a passion. We all know how it feels to be passionate about something that presses all of the right buttons, and the lengths to which we are willing to go to ensure that we spend the maximum amount of time possible doing that very thing.

It stands to reason, then, that if we as leaders can ignite this same passion in our workforce, the benefits will be enormous. People will naturally take more ownership of what they are doing and strive for excellence. Teams will no longer be talking about mere job satisfaction, but about how fulfilling their role in the organisation has become. In relation to the previous chapter, they will be truly **involved**.

By fuelling our people's interest and passion, we create opportunities for the growth and development of the individuals in our teams, building an environment within which they can truly flourish. Levels of involvement, commitment and accountability will be at an all-time high.

Let's take a practical approach to how we are going to go about creating people's interest in their jobs, and keeping that interest at the highest levels possible in the most sustainable way.

HOW TO KEEP PEOPLE INTERESTED

KEYWORDS – EMPOWERMENT AND DELEGATION

We start off by giving our people the maximum amount of autonomy possible in the workplace, which is something we looked at in the previous chapter. What we don't ever want to do is make the terrible mistake of micromanaging.

Micromanagement does not allow people to thrive or flourish in the workplace. It strangles creativity and innovation. Symptoms of micromanaging include, but are not limited to, not allowing people to make even the smallest of operational decisions and certainly not allowing them to participate in the managerial decision-making process (perish the thought). It can also take the form of constant observation of everyone in the workplace, but not in a good way!

We have likely all been micromanaged in some way or another, whether by the teacher who loved using the red pen on our schoolwork to show us the error of our ways, or by the supervisor who constantly peered over our shoulders to ensure that we weren't making a "dreadful mistake", leaving us with no chance whatsoever of being able to focus on what we were doing. If anyone in a position of authority in the modern workplace behaves in this way on a regular basis, they can be absolutely sure that they are creating the conditions for people to fail. I refer to this as **red pen management**, where people are not encouraged to make decisions or, God forbid, be creative, but are told to toe the line and not disrupt the way "things are done around here".

In micromanaged environments, mistakes tend to be treated as abject failures and punished without further consideration of what people can actually learn from them. In fact, the people themselves are treated as failures.

Always remember this pearl of wisdom from motivational speaker and author Zig Ziglar:

"A failure is an event, not a person."

Zig Ziglar[7]

47

This is important for all of us, not only for our own good, but for the good of those we lead. We should not look to catch people out and make them feel like failures. On the contrary, we want to take the advice of the "father" of situational leadership:

"Catch people doing things right."

Kenneth Blanchard[8]

Isn't that how things should be?

If you want people to become and remain interested in what they are doing, you need first and foremost to recognise them for what they are doing **right**. This does not mean that you will never discuss mistakes; it means that you'll see mistakes as an opportunity to learn rather than an excuse to punish.

In an environment with a positive attitude to mistakes, people are more likely to take little risks as they feel safe to fail, as long as they use it as a learning opportunity. These risks, therefore, lead to innovation as they allow people to think for themselves. This is where you can talk about autonomy or people's right to do their job. They feel truly involved with the organisation as they can take decisions about their day-to-day work and tasks without unnecessary and often unwelcome attention or interference from their leaders.

It's here you'll begin to see that interest is a two-way street. If you as leader make every effort to ensure that your employees have the necessary tools and training to do their job, then trust them to get on with it and recognise their achievements, the results are likely to be positive for both them and you. This comes down to the simplest of principles; reciprocity. If you show the right level of interest in what your people are doing, they in turn are more likely to show interest in what you have to say as their leader when you **inform** them and actively look forward to spending time with you. By showing genuine interest in the work and wellbeing of your people, you create **high levels of interest in the work that you do together.**

This is true empowerment through enablement. In other words, you and your team members have created the conditions in which they are able to do their job comfortably.

EMPOWERMENT

What is empowerment? I would describe empowerment as the combination of enablement and autonomy. In other words, not only are team members free to carry out their day-to-day jobs in the best of environments, they also have the confidence and trust of their leaders to deal with exceptional circumstances and situations as and when they arise.

To examine this further, let's take an example. Say there's an excellent employee in a hardware store. He is well known by both his management and by the customers to be one of the very best.

One day, when the management team is off the premises, the most important customer of the store demands a complete refund on a machine worth $2,000. Normally, the employee in question is only authorised to give refunds of up to $200. His brief is to contact his supervisor if he needs to refund a higher amount. However, the supervisor is part of the management team, so is currently unavailable.

Finally, the employee decides to refund the total amount in exchange for the machine. Upon hearing of his initiative, the management team rewards the employee and puts him in line for a promotion.

Why wasn't he punished for non-respect of existing procedures? Well, it might be because the client in question brings $5 million a year in revenue to the store! However, it's more to do with the fact that the management team has created an environment in which team members are encouraged to think for themselves and rationalise the best outcome in any given situation, even if it means breaking the rules.

The store in this example may sound utopian, but why should it be? If people are truly interested in what they are doing and trusted to make decisions in the best interests of their company or organisation, in the vast majority of cases, they will not only do things well, they will do the right things.

DELEGATION

This example leads us nicely on to the subject of delegation. Some people say that delegation is an art in itself, and I would tend to agree with this. For an act of delegation to be successful, it needs to respect numerous criteria.

It may seem obvious, but first of all, you need to make sure that the person to whom you are delegating a task is competent and has the correct skillset to be able to complete it. If you've not made sure of this, you are in effect setting up the delegation and your team member for failure.

You must also ensure that the person is correctly motivated and willing to accept the delegation. What do I mean by correctly motivated? Well, two things, really. The first is that the person is able to self-motivate. Basically, they need to be a self-starter who likes to take on a challenge and doesn't mind being held accountable for tasks, projects or jobs. In other words, they must have the right level of **interest** in taking on the task.

Secondly, they need to have an incentive to do what is being asked of them. This can be a financial incentive, a personal incentive – the task relates to something they are extremely interested in – or an improvement incentive – the task is part of their development or training programme. This last point should be a given, especially when you are in the process of training people to become the managers and leaders of tomorrow.

If your team member has all of the necessary skillsand a great reason to be motivated to do the task, you still need to check that they are prepared to accept this particular delegation. As with objectives, any delegation has to be agreed between all parties concerned.

When you're delegating, be extremely clear with regard to the scope and depth of the task in question. By scope, I mean all the elements and context of the delegation. By depth, I mean the level to which you give the person you're delegating to the authority to act.

Bear in mind that you can give different degrees of authority. If, for example, you give them total authority, this means the team member has the same power of decision as you do in all things related to the project, including the employment of human, material or financial resources.

Partial authority means that under certain circumstances, which you both define and clarify at the beginning of the delegation process, the person needs to check in to obtain your confirmation on a decision before going ahead. Although delegation does imply confidence and trust in your team members, it does not under any circumstances exclude you from retaining a certain amount of control.

Happily, if you are having one-to-one meetings with your team members on a regular basis, this process of control will already be formalised. When you come to delegate, you won't be required to put in place an additional process.

Last, but certainly not least, beware of distributing rather than delegating tasks. This can be a problem, in particular if you're delegating due to your own time constraints, when it can be tempting to hand off tasks to people simply because you don't have the time or interest to do them yourself. Although this can be necessary at times, for example if something is urgent, but not important enough that you need to become directly involved, if distributing tasks becomes the norm, your people will realise that they are being used rather than respected.

Although empowerment and delegation are the most effective ways of maintaining people's interest in what they are doing, they are by no means the only ways. Others include job sharing or rotation, an internal promotion policy or a sustainable learning culture within the organisation. Let's take a closer look at this third point.

SUSTAINABLE LEARNING

When I refer to a sustainable learning culture, I am not only talking about the need for formalised training and development programmes. I'm also talking about a culture of transmission where experienced people mentor and coach their less experienced counterparts, and everyone has an opportunity to expand and share their creativity and innovation.

Leaders who encourage sustainable learning engender true intergenerational and intercultural understanding based on the organisation's mission and vision. They understand the importance and value of diversity and inclusion as well as instilling a constant thirst in their people for education and innovation.

You may have heard of the 70-20-10 model of training. The foundations for this theory were originally laid in the 1980s by Morgan McCall, Michael M. Lombardo and Robert A. Eichinger, while they were researching how successful managers develop over time. The theorywas then further explored in a book by Eichinger and Lombardo published in 1996.[9] One conclusion ofthis research was that 70% of a leader's knowledge is obtained through on-the-job experience and training, 20% through social interaction and only 10% through formal training.

This theory has the merit of giving a holistic approach to learning which recognises that training is only one small aspect relevant to building knowledge and skills. The 70% describes hands-on learning (or learning by doing), with 20% of the credit going to learning throughsocial interaction, such as mentoring, coaching or feedback given to people during one-to-one meetings.

With the advent of social media and online training, some would say the ratio of the three different impacts described in the model has changed. I would argue that maintaining all three (even in different proportions)is fundamentally important when you're reinforcing people's interest in the workplace.

Firstly, this is because variation in the methods you use in training will make it less boring and, therefore, more interesting. Secondly, people have different preferences regarding how they learn and these need to be taken into account if empowerment, delegation and diversity are all truly accepted as essential to the overall organisational culture. Finally, real interest is driven only when people have autonomy, empowerment and delegation.

Now that your people are **informed**, **involved** and **interested**, we move on to keeping them **inspired**. Why is inspiration so important and how do you go about finding its source?

KEEP PEOPLE INSPIRED

WHY KEEP PEOPLE INSPIRED?

If you want to give your absolute best as a manager and a leader and get the absolute best from the people who work with you, then there is nothing that can replace true inspiration. In your search for excellence, nothing even comes close to replacing it.

If you have already succeeded in ensuring that your people are informed, involved and interested, you will have very solid foundations upon which to build inspiration. Inspiration is, if you like, the ever-so-important cherry on the cake. I like to think of inspiration asbeing **the fuel that makes winning and success a possibility**.

Without a shadow of a doubt, people are more focused, efficient and effective when they're inspired. Creativity and innovation become the norm, and positive outcomes and work culture become second nature for your people and your company. In reaching this stage, ensuring everyone is inspired, you practically guarantee success for all in the organisation: you, your managers and your team members!

So, with that in mind, let's have a look at how you go about keeping your people inspired.

HOW TO KEEP PEOPLE INSPIRED

KEYWORDS – RECOGNITION AND MOTIVATION

RECOGNITION

Most of us if we're completely honest with ourselves have a deep-seated thirst for recognition in one form or another. Recognition itself can be more or less to do with who we are or what we do, depending on the circumstances. The "Father of American Psychology", William James, expressed this with power and eloquence:

"The deepest principle in human nature is the craving to be appreciated."[10]

Most of us would recognise these words to be true.

Take a moment to reflect on times when people have let you know how much you are appreciated and recognised, either by telling you or by showing you. Often, this appreciation is enough to inspire you towards action or greater things. Nevertheless, remember that recognition can mean different things to different people and hold more or less importance for them.

Recognition doesn't necessarily mean giving someone a financial bonus or prize for outstanding performance. It is also present in the little things you might do every day, like asking the cleaning personnel how they are on your way to your desk in the morning, or remembering to say thank you to your assistant for making you coffee.

We hear an awful lot about the importance of having a strong employer reputation today. Even if your organisation is great, it will only ever be as great as its best people. Those are the people who truly care, not only about ambitious goals, but about their colleagues' need for appreciation and recognition.

People who truly care become inspirational leaders. However, and this is important to recognise, **it is impossible to inspire others to do better than they believe they can do themselves.**

In that case, just how do you go about inspiring people? What's the secret?

You've already laid the correct foundations for inspiration throughout the preceding chapters. After all, if you are not able to **inform** your people correctly, **involve** them in what the company is doing and maintain their **interest** for their work and the organisation, you are certainly not going to be in a position in **inspire** them in any way.

To inspire, you must be able to recognise people for the unique individuals that they are. This will give you a deep understanding of how to motivate them and promote common goals. What better place to start than with people's **needs**? Before we go on to discuss people's wants, desires and aspirations, it is crucial that we understand more generally what people need.

MOTIVATION

Take a look at the following diagram, inspired by Abraham Maslow's famous hierarchy of needs (Fig 1)[11]

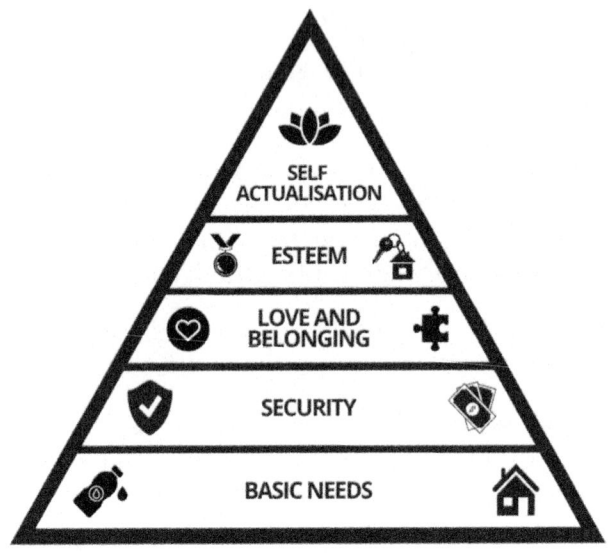

Fig 1. Representation of Maslow's hierarchy of needs

Maslow's model tells us that we all require our needs to be met in a certain order, starting with the most basic physiological ones and climbing all the way up to self-actualisation. This is where inspiration becomes more dependent on our capacity for self-motivation (intrinsic) rather than determined solely by external stimuli (extrinsic).

As the illustration shows, Maslow's hierarchy of needs is often represented as a triangle with the physiological needs at the bottom and self-actualisation at the top. Basically, to reach our **full potential**, we require all of the needs on the first four levels to be met. If we look at each level individually, this makes perfect sense.

The first level deals with basic physiological needs such as food, water, sleep and shelter from the elements. The second level covers the need for safety, which includes both physical and emotional safety, and security. Having enough money to live and a steady job is fundamental here.

The third level is the need for love and belonging. As humans, we tend to have an inherent desire for social interaction. After that need is met, the fourth level is self-esteem. This relates to our need for recogni- tion and appreciation from those who surround us. The fifth and highest level is to do with the need for fulfilling our own internal aspirations through personal development and growth.

As Maslow's model suggests, if you are to understand motivation, you need to understand that people are motivated by many different factors arranged in a specific order. Motivation is highly personal in nature, which underlines the importance of knowing your employees and team members well. Maslow's model gives you a solid foundation upon which to build.

Numerous authors and theorists have written on the subject of motivation since Maslow. One of the most interesting and well-known theories comes from American psychologist Frederick Herzberg: the hygiene/motivator, sometimes called the two-factor theory.[12]

The two-factor theory of motivation basically explains that there are certain things which are sources of dissatisfaction and others which are sources of satisfaction.

HERZBERG'S TWO-FACTOR THEORY OF MOTIVATION

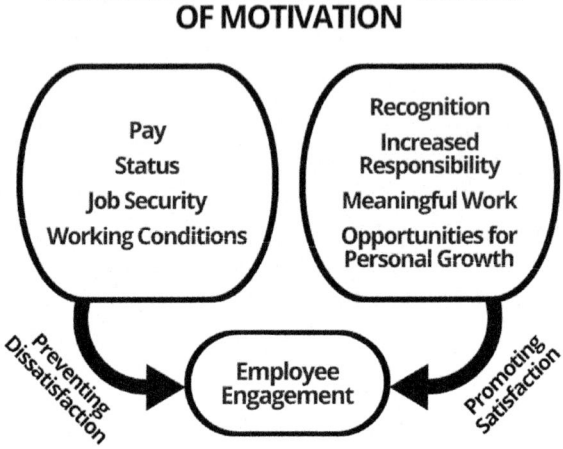

Fig 2. Based on Herzberg's two-factor theory of motivation

Basically, certain factors (the hygiene factors) regularly lead to or are sources of minimum satisfaction, or merely prevent dissatisfaction, while others (the motivator factors) contribute to us being truly satis- fied (or motivated) by what we are doing. Hygiene factors include salary, job security and relationships with others in the workplace. Motivator factors include recognition, a sense of achievement and personal growth.

Herzberg believed that these factors operated independently of one another. He further believed that the hygiene factors would **never be real sources of satisfaction, but only prevent dissatisfaction**, and it was recognition, appreciation and the chance for people to develop themselves that were really responsible for motivation.

In actual fact, the hygiene factors are talking about the first three levels of Maslow's model, the basic needs. The motivator factors refer to the top two of self-esteem and self-actualisation. This means that we can only truly begin the work of inspiring our team members when we have more than adequately dealt with all of their basic needs or hygiene factors – *more than adequately* being the important words here – before going on to talk about self-esteem and self-actualisation.

What if we took the so-called hygiene factors and made them "best in class" compared to our organisa- tion's competitors? In other words, we work on our overall employee reputation by offering people higher levels of job security, along with better salaries, working conditions and guarantees regarding their physical and psychological safety than they could get elsewhere.

As an example, let's say we offer to our workers the opportunity to choose the number of days that they want to work each week and how many hours per day, with a minimum number of three workdays and a maximum number of five. Some people might love a cycle where they work a lot of hours over three days, and then have four days off. Others may prefer to work fewer hours each day over four days with three days off, while another group's preference would be to stick to the traditional eight-hour days, five days a week with a two-day weekend to themselves.

You might think that sounds utopian, but is it really? I actually see it as the next level of empowerment where people have a say in not only what they do and how they do it, but also when they do it.

The point here is that even for the so-called hygiene factors, you can make a big difference in the way your people feel about the workplace and rapidly reduce dissatisfaction towards zero. Indeed, the first two chapters of this book, dealing with keeping people **informed** through better communication and keeping people **involved** through active participation in the life of the organisation, are the logical modern extensions of meeting the hygiene factors.

We have already covered three essential ways to motivate our people by informing, involving and interesting them in the organisation. But what takes people from being well motivated to truly inspired?

Let's first take a look at the difference between the meanings of the words themselves. Motivation can be either extrinsic or intrinsic in nature. It is what drives us to take action to fulfil specific needs at specific times or at whatever stage we find ourselves in our development or learning journey.

Inspiration on the other hand is purely external and has much more to do with a feeling of having been moved or influenced by someone or something else. We can all find inspiration from a wide variety of places and sources, including what we read, the music we listen to, the science and innovation all around us, nature, or own personal interests and passions. I'm sure you know how it feels to be pumped after listening to a particularly stirring piece of music or watching a film which has great significance for you.

We may also be inspired by people we consider to be role models. Inspiration within a workplace is often more to do with leadership and a positive culture than factors such as salary and environment that merely allow us to satisfy our immediate basic needs for safety and belonging.

So, motivation is more about what leads us to take action in any given situation, whereas inspiration deals with attitudes and mindset. On an individual basis, it is important for each of us to find our own purpose in the workplace, but in the creation of a global work culture, positive attitudes and mindsets are being actively promoted as the norm.

If inspiration has a lot to do with leadership and role models, this begs the question: what exactly should we be doing as leaders to **inspire** our people? The single most important thing that we as leaders can do to inspire our people is to **lead by example.** So, the real question if we want to inspire people is what exactly should we be doing to **set an example** to others in the organisation?

To answer that, let's look at what inspirational leaders have in common. The following quote from the well-respected actress, singer and philanthropist Dolly Parton gives us a great starting point:

"If your actions create a legacy that inspires others to dream more, learn more, do more and become more, then, you are an excellent leader."[13]

For people to dream, they require something to dream about, a vision of the future. An inspirational leader must not only have a vision of the future, but also be able to communicate this vision in a compelling way. Then people will be inspired towards achieving goals and objectives aligned with the vision.

Inspirational leaders are often extremely passionate about what they do, and are able to transmit their passion and enthusiasm to those they work with. If you've had occasion to listen to a great leader talking about something they are passionate about, you'll likely have felt the hairs standing up on the back of your neck. Know that feeling? Then you'll know exactly what I'm talking about here!

Another skillset great leaders need is to be able to put themselves in the shoes of others, thereby creating a true emotional connection and level of understanding for what each of their people is experiencing. What

I am talking about here is empathy. Empathy is more important than simply showing concern (or sympathy) for someone's situation or circumstance. Leaders who are truly inspirational have extremely high levels of emotional intelligence and are able to be both empathetic and sympathetic, using both correctly in the right context and at the right time.

Leaders who inspire also tend to have a positive outlook. They see the best in the very worst of situations and are solution rather than problem oriented. This positive energy is often coupled with a good sense of humour:

"There is little success where there is little laughter."

Andrew Carnegie[14]

It goes without saying that a leader who is positive and in good spirits most of the time is a lot easier to approach and communicate with than one who is constantly grumpy or prone to outbursts of temper. Great leaders have the capacity to laugh at themselves and accept that they can make mistakes like everyone else. This shows their people that they believe mistakes and failure are necessary steps on the way to success.

As an inspirational leader, you don't change with the weather. You stay true to yourself, whatever the circumstances, and to do this, you have to know exactly who you are and be happy in your own skin. You have a code of ethics and values which you constantly adhere to; you have integrity.

This, of course, does not mean that great leaders are not able to adapt their management style in response to differing circumstances, contexts or people. What it does mean is that they are happy and confident with who they are, which inspires confidence in others.

"Leadership is a matter of having people look at you and gain confidence, seeing how you react. If you're in control, they're in control."

Tom Landry[15]

If this all describes your leadership style, give yourself a pat on the back! Your people will know that when you make promises, you keep them. This engenders high levels of trust.

You will be growth oriented in three different areas: personal growth (your own), your people's growth (through education and training) and the organisation's growth in its market or industry. This growth mindset is infectious in nature in that it provides a fantastic catalyst for motivation and inspires your people towards higher levels of creativity and innovation.

As an inspirational leader, you will be resilient and able to deal with failure and adversity. You will be determined, tenacious and well disciplined.

"Discipline is the bridge between goals and accomplishment."

Jim Rohn[16]

Resilience, tenacity and discipline enhance the feeling of confidence that your people have in you as their leader, and your authenticity. As an inspirational leader, you will be seen as a facilitator, recognised for your role as coach and mentor. As such, you will be in a position to help people draw their own conclusions and motivate themselves to find their own solutions to problems. That is what being a facilitator is all about: allowing others to bounce ideas off you and guiding them towards the optimum solutions for both themselves and the organisation.

Being an inspirational leader, you will be in the habit of leading from the back most of the time. You'll only lead from the front, i.e. tell people what they must do rather than guide them to make their own informed decisions, when absolutely necessary. Leading from the back emphasises the importance of empowerment and delegation, which goes hand in hand with the role of facilitator. You are there to help your people succeed, putting them in the limelight. Under no circumstances are you there to steal their thunder. As an inspirational leader, you not only create followers, you constantly **involve** them in a process of succession planning, creating the leaders of tomorrow.

So, what about leading from the front? When do you have to do that? This is what I call "the buck stops with me" leadership. Truly inspirational leaders do not apportion blame when things go wrong; you take responsibility for mistakes that your team has made and move on.

This does not mean you don't analyse or debrief with the team to prevent the mistake being made again and improve future performance. What it means is that you as leader are accountable on behalf of the team members and ensure that you protect their integrity at all times.

Last but by no means least, as an inspirational leader, you know how to celebrate your team's success, and never forget to do so. This is so important. It is all too easy to constantly be calling for better and better results in the name of continuous improvement while forgetting to celebrate the little successes that makeup that improvement. At a very basic level, you are reinforcing the types of behaviours which have led you to where you are today.

IT'S A TEAM SPORT

As we have discussed, there are a certain number of qualities which leaders need to display to be considered inspirational. However, never forget that you are also a human being. Although you might have all of the qualities required to be an inspirational leader, you may be stronger in certain areas than in others.

What is truly important here is to know where your strengths and weaknesses lie. As much as possible, listen to your own advice as leader and work to your strengths, just as your team members work to theirs. This reinforces your all-important authenticity.

There is nothing worse than pretending that you are great at absolutely everything! If you were, only your own competence and skillset would be required; no team necessary. However, this is not at all the case. Leadership and management are most definitely team sports.

To inspire, you not only have to have a certain number of qualities, you also need to know where your own strengths lie, be confident in your ability for leadership and, above all, how to lead by example.

KPIs
A NEW APPROACH

CONCLUSION

We began our new approach to KPIs by looking at keeping people **informed**. This is a prerequisite for us as successful leaders in the modern world, allowing us to get people **involved** by encouraging them to participate actively in the organisation while laying the foundations for our CSR policies. This in turn fosters employee involvement on a more global scale.

We then went on to look at how we keep people's levels of **interest** as high as possible. We do this by empowering them within a culture where learning and development are the norms. Real delegation, rather than distribution, is one of the many positive outcomes.

In the final chapter, we discussed people's requirements in the workplace, looking first at their basic needs. We explored the keywords, recognition and motivation, in detail, examining the different factors that could impact either one positively or negatively. All this was backed up by theories from well-respected psychologists Abraham Maslow and Frederick Herzberg.

There is an important difference between motivation and inspiration. It is in actual fact **inspiration** – our ability to influence company culture and promote positive attitudes and mindsets in those who make up the organisation – which allows us to motivate others.

We looked at important sources of inspiration, in particular the role of leaders and how demonstrating certain behaviours and traits can positively impact our people.

We studied a number of different qualities that put us as leaders in a position to inspire the people in our teams and the organisation as a whole. Among these qualities are authenticity, positivity, resilience and the ability to express a clear and compelling vision. We looked at the importance of having a growth mindset on three different levels, personal, managerial and organisational, as well as the need for discipline and accountability. Finally, emotional intelligence, manifesting as empathy and compassion, is essential.

Just like Maslow's model, where people's needs are fulfilled in a specific order, the model for human-centred KPIs needs to follow a certain route. All parts of the model are inherently related. They're interdependent and cannot be viewed in complete isolation.

Without being able to communicate properly with people, we would not be in a position to involve them so they truly participate in the life of the company. If people are not at all involved with what they are doing, we will find it nigh on impossible to maintain their interest. We certainly won't be in a position to empower them or practise delegation. Finally, without information, involvement and interest, it will be very difficult to create an inspirational work culture across the organisation where positive mindsets and attitudes are the expected norms.

The new KPIs are intertwined and interdependent, but at the same time, they build one upon the other. Represented as a diagram similar to Maslow's hierarchy, our model for the new KPIs would look like this:

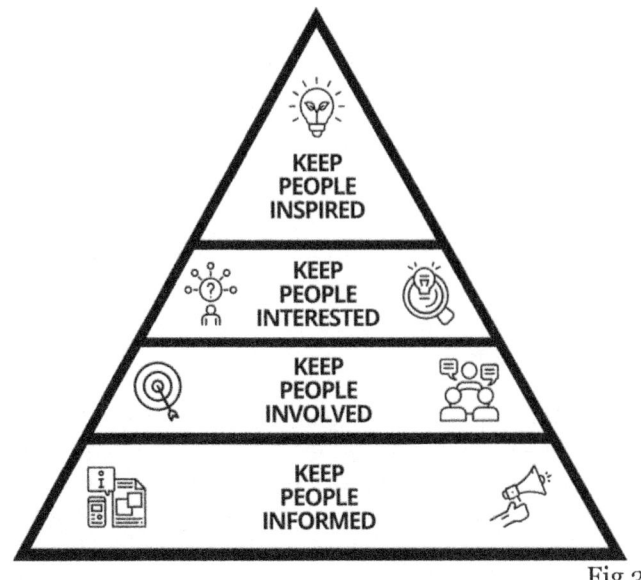

Fig 3

Although all of the new KPIs are important, the ultimate objective is to inspire our people so that they will no longer have too much reliance on external motivation factors and be more self-driven and self-reliant. As leaders, we must truly understand that the people we work with are human beings who all have unique motivations, needs, aspirations and dreams.

Using the building blocks of information, involvement, interest and inspiration will create the conditions for sustainable success in all areas of our business, no matter which of the more traditional KPIs we use to measure this success. To be crystal clear, the KPIs we have been talking about in this book are concernedwith taking human-centric actions to positively affect motivation and the adoption of inspirational leadership behaviours. The new KPIs are **not traditional measures of performance**.

They are, however, **measurable** using tools suchas employee satisfaction, engagement or experience surveys. They can also be measured indirectly, but still highly effectively by looking, for example, at the costs of turnover or the percentage of absences or accidents in the workforce compared to acceptable or normal levels at a given point in time.

Whatever measures you use to look at your organisation's levels of employee engagement or satisfaction, it is crucial you take appropriate action based on the results you observe. Far too often, employee surveys are not given the respect that they deserve, with leaders regarding them as a box-ticking exercise that gets in the way of their relentless pursuit of external client satisfaction. Today, the **most important clients of managers and leaders are in fact their employees.**

There is absolutely no doubt whatsoever that, everything else being equal, organisations that adopt human- and employee-centric strategies and culture will outperform those that do not. Employees who are informed, involved, interested and inspired will naturally be inclined to stay with their organisation, increase the quality of their work and lower their absenteeism. This in turn will raise client satisfaction, leading to loyalty, repeat custom, recommendations, higher revenues, lower operating costs and, in the end, increased market share and profits for your organisation.

Inspiring workers is an ongoing process that requires a proactive approach. You must constantly assess your employees' needs and find the best possible solutions to meet them. As leader, you need to be committed to creating an environment where your people can grow and develop themselves. Your most important concern should always be the wellbeing of your employees.

By unlocking everyone's full potential through informing, involving, interesting and inspiring them, you will make creativity and innovation the rulerather than the exception. As any business leader should know, innovation and creativity are essentialfor companies that wish to thrive in today's somewhat troubled and complex times. Leaders who embrace the new KPIs and put them into practice on a daily basis will set the pace and be instrumental in creating the workplace of the future.

OTHER BOOKS BY THE SAME AUTHOR

THE INCREDIBLE VALUE OF EMPLOYEE POWER UNLEASHED (JUNE 2019)

How to gain competitive advantage by treating your employees well!

One of the biggest problems we are facing in today's workplace is that micromanagement has become the norm. This type of leadership is not only inversely proportional to employee engagement, the two are in fact mutually exclusive.

Both now and in the future, key themes such as autonomy, empowerment and employee engagement will be the foundations upon which companies will build competitive advantage. Confidence and trust will become more and more critical to success, because the key themes rely on them.

This book describes the incredible source of largely untapped power which exists within organisations and companies today, namely employees. This most important resource for any organisation should be treated as such.

Lead the way in the modern business environ- ment! Learn how to make your organisation truly employee-centric.

ONE TO ONE (OCTOBER 2020)

Managing quality time with individuals for engagement and success

Employee engagement is one of the major challenges that companies face today. A lack of engagement results in extremely high costs to organisations in terms of turnover, recruitment and training, as well as a lowering of productivity.

This book demonstrates how you can improve employee engagement through one-to-one meetings. Its clear step-by-step guidance and instructions will show you everything you need to do to run these meetings in the optimum way.

Ultimately, this book demonstrates both how and why effective one-to-one meetings result in additional value for companies, both today and tomorrow. Discover how everyone wins: you as leader, your team members and the organisation as a whole.

TIME TO MANAGE (AUGUST 2022)

An agenda for effective leadership

This is no ordinary time-management book. It is designed to give you all the information you need to create an agenda for effective and successful leadership.

In its pages, you will find a step-by-step guide to ensure you use your own time as leader and that of your team(s) for optimum success. The book will teach you how best to employ time-management and planning tools, making sure you're not only an efficient leader, you're also an effective one. Doing the right things is critical when you're creating the sustainable work environment of the future.

Ultimately, this book will guide you through the types of management and leadership choices you need to make to ensure success. By adopting the techniques and principles we discuss in this book, you will be able to manage your time and create your own unique agenda for effective leadership.

ENDNOTES

[1] Paul J Meyer Quotes. BrainyQuote.com, BrainyMedia Inc, 2023 https://www.brainyquote.com/quotes/paul_j_meyer_190945, accessed 26 April 2023

[2] Bennis, WG; Nanus, B (1985) Leaders: The strategies for taking charge (New York: HarperCollins)

[3] Yang, J; Mufson, C (February 2023) "Why American cities are struggling to supply safe drinking water" (PBSO News Weekend) www.pbs.org

[4] Thackeray Ritchie, A I (1885) Mrs Dymond (London: Smith, Elder & co). Quote from book inspired the quote used in the text, according to the most reliable sources.

[5] Doran, G T (1981) "There's a S.M.A.R.T. way to write management goals and objectives" Management Review, 70 (11):35–36

[6] Stewart, R H (June 2019) The Incredible Value of Employee Power Unleashed – How to gain competitive advantage by treating your employees well (RHS Consulting)

[7] Zig Ziglar Quotes (no date) BrainyQuote.com. Retrieved 17 April 2023, from BrainyQuote.com

Website: https://www.brainyquote.com/quotes/zig_ziglar_378592

8 "How we Lead, conversations on leadership with Ken Blanchard" https://howwelead.org/2014/12/24/catch-people-doing-something-right/

9 Lombardo, M. M.; Eichinger, R. W. (1996) The Career Architect Development Planner (1st ed.) (Minneapolis: Lominger)

10 William James QuotesBrainyQuote.com https://www.brainyquote.com/quotes/william_james_125466, accessed 15 April 2023

11 Maslow, A. H. (1943) "A Theory of Human Motivation". In Psychological Review, 50 (4), 430–437

12 Herzberg, F.; Mausner, B.; Snyderman, B. B. (1959) The Motivation to Work (2nd edition) (New York: John Wiley)

13 Dolly Parton quote from Lorne, A. A. The Most Important Thing I Know (Andrews McMeel Publishing, First Edition 1997)

14 Andrew Carnegie Quotes. BrainyQuote.com, https://www.brainyquote.com/quotes/andrew_carnegie_382305, accessed 26 April 2023

15 Tom Landry Quotes. BrainyQuote.com, https://www.brainyquote.com/quotes/tom_landry_154665, accessed 26 April 2023

[16] Jim Rohn Quotes. BrainyQuote.com, https://www.brainyquote.com/quotes/jim_rohn_109882, accessed 26 April 2023

Printed in Great Britain
by Amazon